j 222
Jo   Jones, Mary Alice

      Bible story of creation

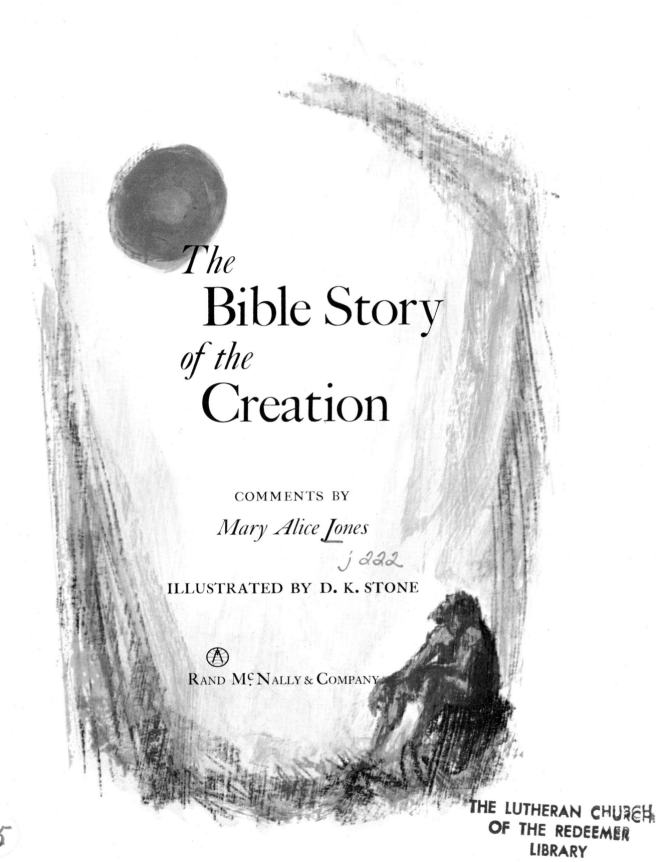

The Bible Story of the Creation

COMMENTS BY

Mary Alice Jones

ILLUSTRATED BY D. K. STONE

RAND McNALLY & COMPANY

The Bible Story of the Creation

Before the mountains were
  brought forth,
Or ever thou hadst formed the
  earth and the world,
From everlasting to everlasting
  thou art God.

Let thy work be manifest to thy
  servants,
And thy glorious power to
  their children.

PSALMS 90:2, 16

IT IS exciting to be alive! To grow and learn; to have questions and to seek answers; to be curious and to explore and experiment so we may satisfy our curiosity about the world.

Through all the ages people of all lands have sought to understand the world in which they live. They have sought to understand themselves as human beings and what they are meant to be and to do.

Big questions all peoples have tried to answer are: How did the world begin? How did life come to be? What is man?

Long, long ago ancient wise men and storytellers and poets and religious leaders tried to express some answers to these questions about the world and how it came to be. Through the years of human history many differing answers have been offered. In our day great men who are historians and great men who are scientists are using all their knowledge and skill to seek more complete answers. Each year they learn more and more about the universe in which they, and you and I, live.

At school you study what they have learned. Sometimes you hear about fresh discoveries over radio and TV newscasts, or read about them in the daily and weekly newspapers. Sometimes you do some serious thinking and some exploring and experimenting yourself. Perhaps one day you may find out something that no one has ever known before about the world and how it came to be. And about man.

The more the historians and scientists make known to us, the more our wonder grows. Wonder at the order and dependability, the vastness and beauty of creation. Scholars who stretch their minds and use all their skills to the uttermost find always there is something more beyond all they have learned. Something science cannot describe nor define.

As men wonder, many of them turn to an ancient account recorded in the first chapter of the Bible. Its language is so beautiful and its rhythm so stately that it is sometimes called the Poem of Creation.

As we read on into the second chapter of the Bible we find some dramatic variations in language. But Genesis 1:1 through 2:3 forms a unit, a poem with a beginning and a conclusion, which men have read with a sense of awe.

The Bible Poem of Creation does not answer all the questions men ask about the beginnings of the universe. It is not a scientific time-line of creation. It speaks of "days" but it does not tell us that the days were bounded by sunrise and sunset as we know them. Indeed, it speaks of "days" before it speaks of sunrise or sunset! As another Bible writer tells us, "With the Lord, one day is as a thousand years, and a thousand years as one day." And yet another one says, "A thousand years in thy sight are but yesterday when it is passed."

The Bible Poem of Creation is unique. It is different from all the other ancient accounts of the beginnings of all things. It has a different purpose from that of present-day scientific writings, a purpose even more important to men. It offers an answer to the primary questions. The Bible Poem of Creation affirms in clear, positive language that the power, the purpose, and wisdom of God are back of all creation, and that creation is good. It is a glorious poem of religious faith written long ago. As we think of it in this way, let us hear what it says to us who live in the world today.

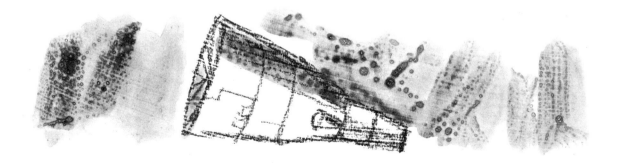

*In the beginning
God created the heavens and the earth.*

GENESIS 1:1

IN THE beginning! The very beginning! The beginning of all that is.

As we try to think of it, our minds reach back, back, back. The historians who study the records ancient men have left on earth, the archeologists who dig up the remains of long-buried civilizations, the biologists who study the fossils of long-ago animals, the geologists who study the formation of rocks, the astronomers who study the sun and moon, the planets, the Milky Way, and the millions of stars—all such thoughtful students have searched the past as far back toward the beginnings as they can go.

Through the years they have learned a great deal about the universe. They have learned that in the dim past suns and heat and energy and water and soil and growing things and living, moving creatures came to be. They have learned something of how through the ages of mighty upheavals and orderly growth the world as we know it today was formed. They have learned the way the planets move, how the seasons come and go. They have learned enough about the movements of winds and clouds to be able to forecast weather and to predict the path of a storm. They have learned of the immensity of the universe, the vastness of space beyond our world, and they have learned more and more about the great laws that hold the universe together.

But of the very beginning, the wisest among men tell us they do not know. How the laws of growth and movement and balance and gravity came to be, they cannot tell. In regard to the very first living cell they have no sure knowledge. The great scientists do not pretend to answer the questions of *why* the universe is orderly instead of meaningless chaos, and *why* its laws can be discovered and depended on by human creatures. For answers to such questions, men leap from science to faith.

Back of all that men have discovered they sense creative power and wisdom and goodness which they cannot measure. As we think about our world we, too, sense that there is something in the universe great beyond our knowing.

From the first inventor of the simplest tool to the man operating the most complex modern computer, from the cave dweller to you and your family living in a home with electric gadgets and appliances, from the first man moving slowly on foot over rough terrain to you in the family car driving over freeways, and to astronauts racing with precision instruments toward the moon—through all the ages of man, human beings have used laws and forces which they did not create but upon which they depend with confidence.

Thus it is that around the world men today affirm their own faith in the words of the ancient Poem of Creation:

> *In the beginning*
> *God created the heavens and the earth.*

Because law and order are in the universe men can depend upon it. We can study it. We can feel sure that as our understanding grows we can know more and more of the truth about creation. The greatness and beauty and order of creation calls us to worship God, the Creator.

And the earth was without
form and void,
And darkness was upon
the face of the deep.
And the spirit of God
was moving over
the face of the waters.

Genesis 1:2

IT IS hard to think of the beginning of all things. It is hard even to wonder about "before-the-universe was." Yet the universe we live in did come to be! And so through the ages thoughtful, inquiring men have sought to find some way in which to express the idea of the beginning of the world they know. Some have expressed it in the language of science. Some have expressed it in the language of history. Some have expressed it in the language of religious faith.

The Bible Poem of Creation pictures the beginning thus:

> *And the earth was without form and void,*
> *And darkness was upon the face*
> *of the deep.*

This is an awesome picture! Darkness, emptiness everywhere.

But this picture of emptiness is not all that is written here. The Bible poem continues:

> *And the spirit of God was moving over*
> *the face of the waters.*

This is what is important in the Bible Poem of Creation. In the very beginning there was the presence of God. Amid nothingness, void and darkness, in the thought of God there was something-to-be. And out of the goodness and purpose of God the universe was born.

17

And God said,
  "Let there be light";
And there was light.
And God saw that the light was good;
And God separated the light
  from the darkness.
God called the light Day,
And the darkness he called Night.
And there was evening and
  there was morning, one day.

GENESIS 1:3-5

IN THE Bible Poem of Creation there is purpose. There is wisdom. There is power. There is goodness. There is God. And God acts.

Then the Bible story of beginnings moves forward. Out of dark nothingness, something was coming to be! There were the stirrings of mighty forces. Creation was in process.

The darkness that was upon the face of the deep did not remain merely darkness. The Poem of Creation says that in the thought of God for creation there was light.

The vast forces that were stirring did not continue shrouded in darkness. Upon the movement of these forces light dawned. Out of darkness came a radiance. The face of the waters gleamed. There was light.

And light was good.

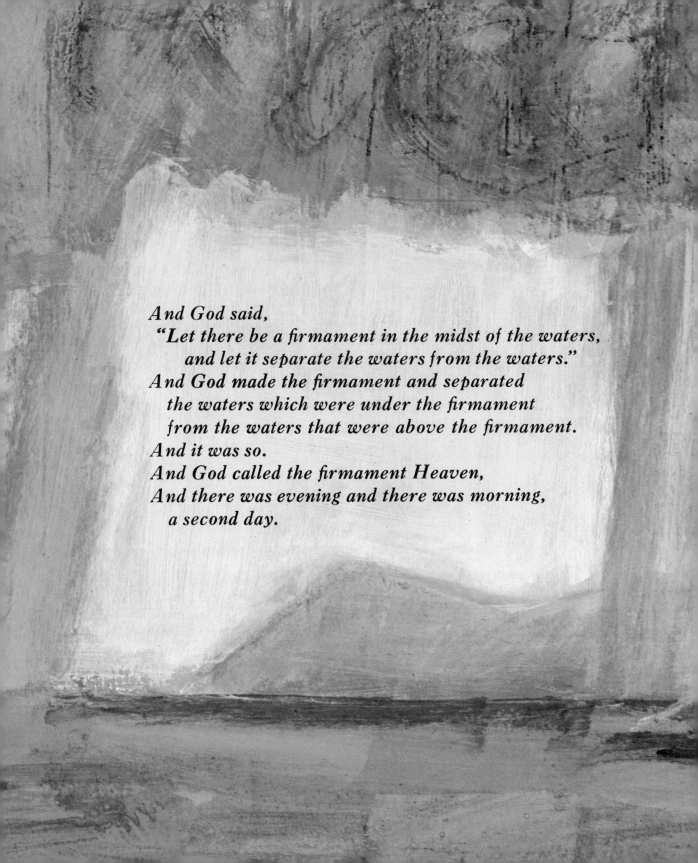

And God said,
  "Let there be a firmament in the midst of the waters,
      and let it separate the waters from the waters."
And God made the firmament and separated
    the waters which were under the firmament
    from the waters that were above the firmament.
And it was so.
And God called the firmament Heaven,
And there was evening and there was morning,
    a second day.

And God said,
 "Let the waters under the heavens
    be gathered together in one place,
    and let dry land appear."
And it was so.
God called the dry land Earth,
And the waters that were gathered together
He called Seas.
And God saw that it was good.

GENESIS 1:6-10

THE Bible Poem of Creation continues the story of the universe-to-be.

Out of emptiness there came something. Out of darkness there came light. Out of stillness there came movement.

The mists over the face of creation were lifting. Out of the steamy fog there came air. Out of the gloomy shadows there came form. There were mighty movements. The waters were gathered together. Vast seas were moving in waves tipped with light. The air became clear. Above there was the firmament, the vaulted arch of the skies, against which luminous clouds trailed, continually changing their shape.

Steadily, majestically within the purpose of God, creation was moving forward. But a world of sea and sky was not enough. Its vastness was monotonous.

The Bible Poem of Creation speaks now of Earth. We

think today of the Earth as the planet upon which we live.
Here, in the midst of the water, something more was coming
to be. The waters no longer heaved restlessly. As the waves
broke, they dashed upon a shore. Substance was there. Land
had come to be! Land with all its possibilities for the future.

Thus, the Bible poem tells us, out of dim mists and emptiness there had come to be form and color, a world of sea
and sky and land. Out of watery swamps, mountains and
valleys and plains appeared. The land became dry and firm.
Around the land the seas flowed in constant motion. And
over the land were the clear air and the blue sky and the
white clouds.

The world was coming to be! God's presence was making itself felt. God's thought was taking form in creation.
God's thought for a good world.

And God said,
  "Let the earth put forth vegetation,
    plants yielding seed
    and fruit trees bearing fruit
    in which is their seed,
    each according to its kind,
    upon the earth."
And it was so.
The earth brought forth vegetation,
    plants yielding seed according to
    their own kinds,
And trees bearing fruit
    in which is their seed,
    each according to its kind.
And God saw that it was good.
And there was evening and
    there was morning,
    a third day.

GENESIS 1:11-13

THE Bible poem tells of new glories that came to be—greater than all that had gone before.

The vast movements were becoming still. The world seemed to be waiting.

Then growing things came to be!

The Bible Poem of Creation tells us that God's thought was not for a world finished at a given time, flung out into space, forever unchanged. It was for something more wonderful. It was for a dynamic world, a world which had within itself power to continue to grow, to become ever more fruitful, to change. It was for a world, not merely boundless and massive, but alive!

The thought of God included tiny cells of life as well as wide seas. It included the smallest seed as well as the greatest mountain. The seeds had within them the energy to grow and become grass and herbs and fruit trees. The plants and trees bore more seed so that there could be more and more and more plants and trees, always growing, always changing, renewing themselves year after year.

There was life in the world! Life that would increase, so that creation could go on through all the ages.

And God saw that it was good.

And God said,
"Let there be lights in the firmament of the heavens
    to separate the day from the night;
    and let them be for signs and for seasons
    and for days and years,
    and let them be lights in the firmament of the
    heavens to give light upon the earth."
And it was so.

GENESIS 1:14-15

THE Bible poem moves on to times and seasons. Creation was not to be a dull sameness. There was to be day and night, and seasons and years.

In God's thought for creation there was to be rhythm; light and darkness; growing time and fruit-bearing time; heat and cold. There was to be growth and change. From day to day, from season to season, from year to year.

One day a seed would be upon a tree; another day it would lie upon the ground. One season it would seem dead, a tiny, dry bit of substance resting quietly in the soil that had been planned to receive and nourish it. The next season it would be alive, bursting into fresh green leaves. One year it would be a tiny plant; another year a sturdy tree, bearing its own seeds.

In the plan of God

> *While the earth remains,*
> *Seed time and harvest, cold and heat,*
> *Summer and winter, day and night,*
> *Shall not cease.*
>
> GENESIS 8:22

And God made two great lights,
The greater light to rule the day,
And the lesser light to rule the night;
He made the stars also.
And God set them in the firmament
   of the heavens
To give light upon the earth,
To rule over the day
   and over the night,
And to separate the light
   from the darkness.
And God saw that it was good.
And there was evening
   and there was morning,
   a fourth day.

GENESIS 1:16-19

WE MAY wonder why the Bible Poem of Creation speaks of day and night before it speaks of the sun and moon; why it speaks of growing things before it speaks of seasons. Rather than being a time-line of creation, the Bible poem is an affirmation that all that came to be came from the thought and purpose and goodness of God. It tells us that all that is, is dependent upon God, and that creation is good.

The poem tells us that law and dependability were part of creation. Thus slowly out of disorder came order. The sun served its purpose as a center of light and warmth. The planets moved in their orbits. The stars took their appointed places.

The world became a part of a law-abiding universe, established in the purpose of God.

But this was not all. There came bright sunlight and a deep blue sky; quiet moonlight on silver clouds; twinkling stars against a velvet night. There came waving green leaves on towering plants; flowering vines on a hillside, ripening fruit on low-bent trees.

There was beauty in the world! And it was good.

And God said,
  "Let the waters bring forth
    swarms of living creatures,
    And let birds fly above the earth
      across the firmament
      of the heavens."
So God created
    the great sea monsters and
    every living creature that moves,
    with which the waters swarm,
    according to their kinds,
    and every winged bird
    according to its kind.

And God saw that it was good.
And God blessed them, saying,
  "Be fruitful and multiply,
    and fill the waters in the seas,
    and let the birds multiply
    on the earth."
And there was evening and
    there was morning,
    a fifth day.

GENESIS 1 : 20-23

FROM dead nothingness God's thought and purpose for creation had brought light, life, and growth.

There had been movements of great forces out of which had come the sea and the sky and the land. There had been gentle movements of growing grasses and trees, rooted in the soil. There had been the stately movements of the heavenly bodies, following the laws planned for them. There had been the silent movement of the seasons, one after another, in orderly sequence.

Now the Bible Poem of Creation describes a new sort of movement. Living creatures were moving in the sea. Birds were flying between the earth and sky. Their paths were not fixed and unchanging. There came to be creatures whose movements were not bound by dependence upon rocks in the sea or upon roots in the soil. They were free to move. They filled the earth and the seas around them with color and swift, graceful movement.

Within the purpose of God, creation was moving forward.

And it was good.

And God said,
  "Let the earth bring forth living creatures
     according to their kinds;
     Cattle and creeping things and beasts of the earth
     according to their kinds."
And it was so.
And God made the beasts of the earth
     according to their kinds
     and the cattle according to their kinds,
     and everything that creeps upon the earth
     according to its kind.
And God saw that it was good.

GENESIS 1: 24-25

LIFE and ever more life! Life in seed becoming grass and herbs; life in cells becoming fish and birds and animals that move. Life firmly rooted in the soil, swimming in the seas surrounding the land, life flying in the air about the earth, life creeping and walking upon the ground!

Yet creation did not move in haste. The living creatures in the sea did not come until the sea was ready for them. The birds did not come until the land was ready for them. The grasses and trees did not come until the soil was ready for them. The animals did not come until the ground was ready for them.

For all new life that came there was preparation. It all came according to the purpose and the power of God. God's thought was for a world in which there would be order and dependability, where new life would be able to grow and in-

crease and move forward because the world was ready for it when it came. A world in which each kind of life could grow according to the laws planned for it, and so be ready to change to meet its needs as creation moved forward.

Slowly, surely, God's purposes were coming to be in life that was ever more varied, life that was ever more beautiful, more fruitful, more free.

But there was yet more to come. All the work of creation that had gone before was not enough. The earth and the sea and the sky; the sun and the moon and the stars; the grass and the herbs and the trees; the fish and the birds and the creeping things and the animals that walk upon the earth —all this was not enough.

God's greatest thought and purpose for his creation was yet to be realized.

Then God said,
  "Let us make man in our image,
    after our likeness;
    and let them have dominion
    over the fish of the sea,
    and over the birds of the air
    and over the cattle, and over all the earth,
    and over every creeping thing
    that creeps upon the earth."
So God created man in his own image,
  in the image of God he created him;
  male and female he created them.
And God blessed them, and God said to them,
  "Be fruitful and multiply,
    and fill the earth and subdue it;
    and have dominion over the fish of the sea
    and over the birds of the air
    and over every living thing that moves
    upon the earth."

And God said,
　"Behold, I have given you
　　　every plant yielding seed
　　　which is upon the face of all the earth,
　　　and every tree with seed in its fruit;
　　　you shall have them for food.
　　And to every beast of the earth
　　　and to every bird of the air,
　　　and to everything that creeps
　　　upon the earth,
　　　everything that has the breath of life,
　　I have given every green plant for food."
And it was so.

GENESIS 1: 26-30

IN GOD's purpose for creation there was something more than grandeur and life and beauty and fruitfulness. In his purpose there were minds that could share his thoughts for all creation; hearts that could love him. There were creatures who could dream of future goods and work with God in bringing them to be.

And so man came to be upon the earth. Man in the image of God. That is, man who could think God's thoughts after him, man who could have fellowship with him, respond to his concern and love. Man who could learn and plan and work.

All that was needful for the making of a beautiful and fruitful and good world was ready. Now the God of all creation called man to be his helper. Into man's hands God entrusted the earth. To "subdue" it and "have dominion over"

it; to explore the universe, to seek to understand it, and to use it, and to use the world and all its rich possibilities in accordance with God's good purpose.

More than this, God set man free. Free to make choices about how he would live in the world and how he would use all God's gifts.

The Bible Poem of Creation shows us that God's thoughts for man were very great thoughts. In another Bible poem we read:

Thou hast made him little less than God,
And dost crown him with glory and honor.
Thou hast given him dominion over the
works of thy hands.

PSALMS 8:5, 6a

And God saw everything that he had made,
and behold, it was very good.
And there was evening and there was morning,
a sixth day.

GENESIS 1:31

THE Bible Poem of Creation says that creation is good.

There is much in the world today we do not understand. There is much that seems to us not good. There are great convulsions in nature, like tornadoes and hurricanes and earthquakes. There are diseases which cause children to die and there are famine and drought and cruelty and war. We ask, "Why? Why in God's good creation can such terrible things be?"

Though we are learning more and more about our world, no man can give an absolute, final answer to these questions.

We look at all the beauty in the world we know. We consider the provisions for our needs: food and air and water, night and day, summer and winter, and families to love us. We think of all the ways men have worked to make the earth beautiful and fruitful and good. We remember the men who have studied and experimented to learn how to prevent and to cure sickness. We recall those who have struggled to overcome injustice and cruelty and war.

Then we make a leap of faith. Faith in God. Though there are ugliness and suffering and evil yet in the world, God's creation *is* good.

Though men misuse their freedom, a world could not be good without freedom. God's purpose for man *is* good, and man can fulfill it.

Thus the heavens and the earth were finished,
and all the host of them.
And on the seventh day God finished his work
which he had done,
And he rested on the seventh day from all his work
which he had done.
So God blessed the seventh day and hallowed it
because on it God rested from all the work
which he had done in creation.

GENESIS 2:1-3

THE Bible Poem of Creation has been called "The Poem of the Seven Great Days." The six "days" were filled with mighty acts. The last "day" of which the poem tells, the seventh day, is described as a day of rest. "God rested on the seventh day from all his work."

This great Poem of Creation was written long, long ago. We do not know just what it means to tell us when it says that God rested. We know God does not "rest" as we rest. We know it has always been true as it is true today that

He who keeps you will not slumber.
PSALMS 121:3b

But all the children of God do need to rest. They need to worship. And so, in the plan of God, there was to be rest as well as work. There was to be time when regular work would be put aside, when men and women and boys and girls could think without interruption of the world God planned, and of how they can carry out God's purposes for them and for all his creation.

For God did not leave man alone in his world. Through all the ages from the beginning until now God has been working in his world. Through all the ages and from now into eternity God will be working still.

Without God's presence in the world, man could not live. Without man's cooperation in the purposes of God, man cannot have a good life for himself nor help others to have a good life. God and man working together! We believe this is God's plan for his world and for us, whom he calls to be responsible and to share his purposes.

The Bible Poem of Creation is a great affirmation of faith. Of faith in God's mighty power, his purpose for his creation and his high expectations and loving concern for us, his human creatures.

Thus as we seek to find answers to our big questions about our world and how it came to be, we shall stretch our minds with the great scientists and learn all they can tell us. But we shall not stop there. We shall hear back of all they can teach us a call to worship. A call to worship God, the Almighty Creator, who also cares for each one of us.

Serve the Lord with gladness!
Come into his presence with singing!
Know that the Lord is God!
It is he that made us, and we are his;
We are his people and the sheep of his pasture.
Give thanks to him, bless his name.
For the Lord is good;
His steadfast love endures forever,
And his faithfulness to all generations.

PSALMS 100: 2, 3, 4, 5

PRINTED IN U.S.A.